Min

Make You

*Other titles by J.H. Brennan available in Armada*

Mindpower 1
Succeed at School

*The Barmy Jeffers series*
Barmy Jeffers and the Quasimodo Walk
Return of Barmy Jeffers and the Quasimodo Walk
Barmy Jeffers and the Shrinking Potion

Monster Horrorshow

Shiva

Mindpower 2

# Make Yourself a Success

J. H. Brennan

An Armada Original

*Make Yourself a Success* was first published in Armada in 1990

Armada is an imprint of the Children's Division,
part of the Collins Publishing Group,
8 Grafton Street, London W1X 3LA

© 1990 J. H. Brennan

Printed and bound in Great Britain by
William Collins Sons & Co.Ltd, Glasgow

Conditions of Sale
This book is sold subject to the condition
that it shall not, by way of trade of otherwise,
be lent, re-sold, hired out or otherwise circulated
without the publisher's prior consent in any form
of binding or cover other than that in which it is
published and without a similar condition
including this condition being imposed
on the subsequent purchaser.

# CONTENTS

1. The Way to Use This Book — 7
2. One Small Step Towards Getting Everything You've Ever Wanted — 9
3. How to Calculate Your Chances of Success — 16
4. Meet the Monster Lurking in Your Mind — 23
5. Introducing the Sleeping Giant Willing to Help Out in Everything You Do — 29
6. How the Sleeping Giant Can Help You — 34
7. How to Use the Dreaming Giant — 40
8. Your Colour Countdown for Complete Control — 49
9. How to Wake the Sleeping Giant — 61
10. The Magic of Music — 72
11. How the Sleeping Giant Can Help You Do the Impossible — 77
12. Getting Your Self Image into Shape — 84
13. How to Hire the Sleeping Giant as Your Sports Coach — 90
14. Introducing the Advisor Within — 101
15. The Nine-Point Checklist that Turns Desires into Goals and Helps Them Come True — 107
16. The Secret of the Final Secret — 120

Appendix 1. Special Relaxation Exercise — 123
Appendix 2. Special Music — 127

# The Way to Use This Book

Let's get a few things straight from the start. You can't mess about with a book like this.

You either work it –– work your way through the various exercises and techniques — or you dump it.

Just reading it is not enough. That's like trying to build up your muscles by reading a book on weight-lifting.

So when there's a test in this book, do it. Do it seriously and do it right.

And when there's a technique in this book, use it. Take time to practise it until you get the knack, then use it when you need it.

Don't try to swallow the whole book in one go. Take time to absorb the info. Take time to practice the techniques. The changes you want to make in your self will come gradually. But they'll come.

Those are simple instructions. If you follow them you'll benefit. A lot.

One more thing. Throughout, I've tried to explain why things work. It's best you understand these explanations, but if you don't, don't worry: you can still make good use of the techniques.

You don't have to know how a television set works to watch one.

# One Small Step Towards Getting Everything You've Ever Wanted

Have you thought what you want right now?

A new bike? A new sweater? A personal computer? A thousand pounds?

Maybe what you want is more spread out. Maybe you want to do better at school. Maybe you want to fall in love.

Or maybe you're just confused.

You're not alone. I know this sounds weird, but a lot of people — maybe even most people — scrabble through life without ever deciding what it is they want.

They have a vague idea all right.

They vaguely think they'd like a lot of money (without knowing how much.)

They vaguely think they'd like a bigger house (without knowing where.)

They vaguely think they'd like a different career (without knowing what.)

But vague isn't good enough. Vague is like walking into a Travel Agency and asking for an airline ticket to somewhere.

'Where exactly do you want to go?' the clerk asks.

'Just somewhere,' you say. 'Somewhere nice.'

But that doesn't get you somewhere nice. That doesn't get you anywhere at all. If you're going to get the things you really want from life, you need to know exactly what they are.

Which is where your mindpower training starts.

Mindpower is a system for changing a lot of the things that are wrong with your life...by changing the way you think.

One of the things wrong with your life right now is that

you don't have everything you want. I'm not saying you're greedy — I'm just saying there are things you'd like that you just don't have. Can changing the way you think change that? Too right it can!

And here is where you start to prove it.

Some mindpower techniques are pretty weird (as you'll see later in this book) but all you need for this one is a pen and paper. Find a quiet room, sit down, think carefully and make a list of everything you need right now.

Maybe you need a particular book for school. Put that down. Maybe you need a new coat. Put that down. Maybe you need the money for a bus pass because you lost the old one. Put that down too.

I'm not talking what you *want* — I'm talking what you *need*. Nobody *needs* a gold-plated Yamaha or a CD player crafted from a single diamond.

But there are definitely things you do need and need now. You know what they are if you're prepared to think about it. Take as much time as you want to list them all. Try to make sure you don't miss any.

Don't get bogged down wondering if you really need something. If you reckon you need it — and you need it now — that's good enough: include it in your list.

One more thing. Don't leave anything out just because you can't afford it. Or your parents can't afford it. If you need it, put it down whether you can afford it or not.

Head the list:

### THINGS I NEED.

When you've finished making that list, put it to one side and start to make a second list. Head this one:

### THINGS I WANT.

Writing down things you want is usually a lot more fun than writing down things you need. Open your mind right up for this one. Put down everything you want now and everything you think you *might* want sometime in the future.

Don't worry if the things you want are silly and certainly don't worry about how much they cost. If you fancy flying your own jet plane, put down 'jet plane'. If you think it might be nice to own a Medieval castle where you could play *Dungeons & Dragons*, put down 'Medieval castle'.

Whatever things you want, put them down.

It's important to be serious about this. When you get into things like jet planes and Medieval castles, you might be tempted to imagine what you're doing is making a fun list and nothing else.

But you're not. Listing what you want — whatever it is you want — is just as important, just as serious, as listing the things you need. So please do think about it carefully and take as much time as you have to so that nothing you want is left off that list.

When you've finished listing all the things you want, put the list aside and start a third list. Head this one:

## SKILLS, TALENTS, QUALITIES
## I NEED

This list might be a bit more tricky. It requires you to look very closely at yourself and it requires you to be very honest with yourself.

You know the sort of personal qualities that would help you cope a little better. Maybe a talent for Maths would help. Or courage. Or skill at dressmaking.

Stare out the window, think long and hard about yourself, then list down all the skills, talents and personal qualities you know in your heart you need to do the things you have to do these days.

When you've finished that list, put it to one side and start a fourth list. Head it:

## SKILLS, TALENTS, QUALITIES I WANT

In this list, write down those personal qualities, skills and talents you may not necessarily need, but you would like to have anyway.

For example, I doubt you'd ever *need* to be able to turn somersaults on a tightrope, but if you fancy having that particular talent, put it down.

Once again think carefully about the skills, talents and

personal qualities you want and list them.

It may be that you'll need more than one session to complete all four lists. That's okay. If you can't finish them today, come back tomorrow and the day after and the day after that, if necessary. Take as much time as you need.

The important thing is to do a thorough, serious job of creating those four lists.

When you're finished — really finished — you're entitled to congratulate yourself. Because, according to a basic mindpower principle, *knowing* what you want is the first step towards *getting* what you want.

Keep all four of your lists in a private place. Show them to nobody. Tell nobody they exist. But keep them safe, because you'll be getting back to them later.

For now, however, having decided what it is you really want, the time has come to find out what your chances are of getting it.

# How to
# Calculate Your
# Chances Of Success

Test coming up.

This test is different from the sort of tests you take at school. It's more important for one thing.

Take time over it. Think very carefully — *very* carefully — before you answer each question. Most of all, be honest.

Being honest isn't all that easy. Because the test is about *you*. Which means there's always the temptation to massage the facts a little, to make yourself look just that bit better than you really are.

So before you start, make yourself a promise. Promise you will never, ever, show the results of this test to anyone. Not your folks, not your friends, not your teachers.

This test is about you and for you. You alone. It is

absolutely private. So you can be as honest as it takes, because nobody (except you) is ever going to know how you scored.

Keep the result carefully. None of this eat-after-reading or reduce-to-ashes nonsense. Stash it away somewhere safe where only you can find it..

Go to it.

## THE MINDPOWER PERSONAL POTENTIAL TEST

Here's your Personal Potential Calculator. Listed on it are ten Personal Potential Areas (PPAs, for short.)

### PERSONAL POTENTIAL CALCULATOR

PPA 1     **Earning power**                     []

PPA 2     **Getting along**                     []

PPA 3     **Leadership**                        []

| PPA 4 | Leisure skills | [] |
| PPA 5 | Family relationships | [] |
| PPA 6 | Work skills | [] |
| PPA 7 | Persuasive power | [] |
| PPA 8 | Luck | [] |
| PPA 9 | Intelligence | [] |
| PPA 10 | How others see you | [] |

After each PPA, write in, using the space provided (or on a separate sheet of paper if you'll find that easier to hide) how you would rate yourself on a scale of 0 to 100.

At the bottom end, a rating of 0 means you're absolutely useless in the PPA in question, literally the world's worst.

A rating of 50 means you're about average, no better and no worse than most other people.

If you mark yourself 100, it means you consider yourself the best in the world in that area — nobody, but nobody, is better than you.

Let's go through those PPAs one at a time before you rate yourself.

**PPA 1** - Earning power. How do you rate your ability to make money? If you think you're absolutely incapable of ever earning a single penny anywhere at any time, rate yourself zero. If you reckon you're about average, rate yourself 50. If you think you're the world's greatest little earner, multi-millionaire standard, rate yourself 100. Or, more likely, rate yourself somewhere in between.

What we're looking for is your rating of yourself. Think about it very carefully. With the calculator, it's your opinion that counts. Be brutally honest with yourself — remember, no-one will ever see the results of this test but you.

**PPA 2** - Getting along. How well do you think you get alone with people — pretty badly ... about average ... better than average? Rate yourself between zero and 100 in the space provided.

**PPA 3** - Leadership. What's your potential for taking charge? I'm not saying you actually have to take charge all the time, but if you wanted to, how well do you think you'd manage? Rate yourself.

**PPA 4** - Leisure skills. These are the things you do in your spare time. Reading ... crochet ...sports ... guitar ... frog racing ...whatever. Mark yourself on a scale of 0 to 100 on how well, or badly, you do the things you do.

**PPA 5** - Family relationships. How well do you get on with your folks. If you're always hassling, mark yourself low. If you never had a fight with your family in your life, mark yourself high. Remember, it's your opinion that counts.

**PPA 6** - Work skills. Are you top of the class? Middle? Bottom? Work skills aren't confined to school. Maybe you have a talent for fixing cars in your spare time, or sewing leather patches onto jeans. If it's work, put it in the pot, then decide where on a scale of 0 to 100 you come in your ability to do it all well.

**PPA 7** - Persuasive power. So are you a silver-tongued charmer able to chat the birds out of the branches? Or does nobody ever do what you want? Rate your powers of persuasion in the space provided, 0 to 100.

**PPA 8** - Luck. Are you lucky? Do you find money in the street? Did you lose your boarding pass to the Titanic? Do you lead a charmed life? Do things just naturally go right for you? Or are you one of the ones who only get sick on holidays? You know your level of luck. Quantify it on a scale of 0 to 100 in the space provided.

**PPA 9** - Intelligence. If you are the stupidest human being on earth, score zero. If you could eat Einstein for breakfast, score 100. Wherever you think you come on the scale, write it down.

**PPA 10** - How others see you. This one is tricky. This is your opinion of the opinions others hold about you. If you think they think you stink, mark low. If you think they think you're the most wonderful, marvellous, terrific person in the world, score high. You decide what they've decided and rate yourself accordingly.

That's the hard bit. Now comes the maths. Add up all ten scores and write the total down here:

**Total:** _____

The figure you've written down will fall somewhere between zero and 1,000. (I know that because I scored high on PPA 9.) Now divide that figure by ten. When you've done so, write your answer down here:

**Total/10 = _____**

The figure you have just written down will fall somewhere between zero and 100. That figure, which you should keep secret, is your Personal Potential Percentage, sometimes called your P3 for short.

I'll tell you something very interesting about your Personal Potential Percentage in the next section.

# Meet the Monster Lurking in Your Mind

I don't know what you scored for your Personal Potential Percentage (P3) but I can tell you one thing:

It isn't high enough.

Even though I don't know your P3 and I don't know you, I still know, for sure, your Personal Potential Percentage isn't high enough.

I don't mean it *should* be higher. I mean it actually *is* higher. But you didn't know that, so you sold yourself short and calculated the whole thing too low.

Everybody calculates their P3 too low. Let me give you a couple of examples.

When I was in my teens, my best friend was a genius. That's not an exaggeration. He went on to become one of the world's top five nuclear physicists.

But even in the days I knew him, you could see he was something special. At school he was top of the class in everything but Art. He could calculate Maths in his head faster than the teacher could manage on the blackboard. He was so advanced in physics they gave him special lessons so the rest of us wouldn't hold him back.

In his senior year he was School Captain and Sports Captain.

And in all the time I knocked about with him, he thought he was useless.

Oddly enough, the next smartest kid I ever knew thought she was useless too. She was the only one who could hold a candle to my budding physicist at schoolwork. Like him, she sailed through exams while the rest of us sweated. Like him, she had a bright future assured.

But her Mum once told me she worried herself sick all the time. However often she did well at something (which was pretty often) she never believed she could still do it next time around.

Like my friend the physicist, she rated her P3 far below what it actually was.

At the time I knew these two, I thought they were pretty weird. Now I know better. Now I know just about everybody underrates themselves. And a lot of people underrate themselves badly.

My guess is you underrate yourself as well. The Personal Potential Percentage you just calculated is far too low.

The reason it's too low is there's a monster lurking in your mind. That monster's called a *negative self image*.

By now you may have figured what the test was all about. It wasn't really to find your Personal Potential Percentage at all. It was to find out what you *thought* your P3 might be, which is a different thing altogether.

Your actual P3 depends on your mind, your personality, your skills and talents. What you think your P3 might be only depends on your self image.

It wasn't lack of talent that made my teenage friends think they were useless — they had talent coming out of their ears. It was their self image.

Self image is the way you see yourself, the way you imagine yourself to be.

If somebody asks you if you're good-looking, your self image is what determines whether you answer yes or no. The same thing goes for the way you answer questions about whether you're intelligent, witty, successful, charming, attractive and so on.

Everybody's stuck with a particular self image, but very few people ever stop to wonder where it came from. In fact, it started growing when you were very young.

I know you're not exactly ancient now, but I'm talking about *very* young. The days when you couldn't take three steps without wetting yourself. The days when you couldn't read or tell the time. Nobody paid any attention to you unless you fell over.

Because you weren't up to much in those days, your self image wasn't up to much either ... quite rightly so. If you thought of yourself as pretty awful, it was no more than the honest truth.

But then life played a really rotten trick on you. You started to grow up, but your self image didn't.

Don't get me wrong: it changed all right. You certainly see yourself differently now to the way you saw yourself at the age of eighteen months.

But self image builds in layers, like an onion. Whatever you put on top, the centre stays the same. And at the centre is the notion you're a weak, clumsy, powerless, smelly little idiot who's a nuisance to everybody. Because that's the way you used to be.

Of course, you don't think about it that way. You only know you don't feel all that good about yourself. The reason stays hidden almost all the time. It's like a monster lurking in your mind.

I don't want to get complicated about this, but you need to know there's more inside your head than you imagine. The monkey that chatters to you throughout the day is only one small bit of your whole mind.

Underneath the part you know about is a whole area you don't. The experts call this your *unconscious mind*.

A lot of stuff goes on in your unconscious mind. It looks after your heartbeat. It's where your dreams come from. It's where your memories are stored when you're not actually remembering them.

It's also home to the monster.

So if you want to change your self image, you have to find a way of making contact with your unconscious mind.

Which brings us back to mindpower.

# Introducing the Sleeping Giant Willing to Help Out in Everything You Do

The experts say your mind is like an iceberg: only one tenth is above the surface.

That means at very most you only use one tenth of your total brainpower. The rest of it lumbers about doing its own thing.

The part beneath the surface is what we've been calling your unconscious mind. Somebody once described it as a sleeping giant.

That gives you the impression of something huge and powerful, something that could kick sand in a bully's face, leap tall buildings in a single bound.

Which is actually not too far from the truth.

The sleeping giant, your unconscious mind, really is enormously powerful. Take Mozart, for example.

Mozart was playing the harpsichord at the age of three. Two years later he has started his career as a composer by writing a couple of minuets. By the age of eight, he had a full symphony going.

From that point until his early death, his musical output was enormous — and of a quality that established his reputation as one of history's great composers.

But if you ever have an opportunity to examine any of Mozart's original musical manuscripts, you may notice something odd. Although he made only one copy of each score, there are no corrections.

When the average composer creates a symphony, the work goes through several drafts. You write a few chords, try them out on the piano to see how they sound, then change them around until they are exactly right.

But Mozart was not your average composer. He got it right first time ... every time.

He was able to do this because he heard the music in his head, all of a piece. Composing, for him, was simply a question of listening to that imaginary symphony and writing it down.

The question is, if Mozart didn't create the symphony, then who did? The answer is, the sleeping giant. Mozart's works were composed by his unconscious mind.

The giant has created many other works, including *Dr Jekyll and Mr Hyde* for Robert Louis Stevenson and *Frankenstein* for Mary Shelley. These books came up from their authors' unconscious minds in dreams.

But the giant's talents aren't just artistic.

The history of science and technology is full of examples of the sleeping giant at work. Dreams ... hunches ... visions ... intuitions have solved problem after problem.

But the most remarkable example of the sleeping giant at work was in the mind of Nikola Tesla.

Although he's almost forgotten now, Tesla was one of the most amazing inventors in the entire history of humanity. He produced so many things that influence the way we live today that one of his biographers called him 'the man who invented the Twentieth Century.'

Tesla had a very visual mind. He could imagine things so strongly that he actually had difficulty telling the difference between them and reality.

Over the years, he formed a remarkable partnership with his sleeping giant — so much so that when he invented a new piece of machinery, he could build a working model in his imagination, set it running, then examine it days, weeks or months later for signs of wear on its moving parts!

This would be pretty unbelievable if he had not proved it time and again. But the question obviously arises, who kept the machine running while Tesla got on with other things?

You're right, of course — the sleeping giant.

The sleeping giant can make you ill and make you well. It can give you talents you never dreamed you had. It can break your bad habits and help you build up good ones.

It can make your work easier and your play more fun. It

can make you more popular and help you do things you thought were impossible. It can keep your weight under control and earn you money.

Some people even think it can rearrange certain situations for your benefit ... what's usually called 'getting lucky'.

The point about all this is, the sleeping giant is on your side. It's part of you and it's quite prepared to help you. In fact, it actively wants to help you do the things you want to do, be the things you want to be.

Mindpower is really just persuading the sleeping giant to wake up and give you a helping hand.

How well you do that determines how much more of your mind you will use in the future. But if you manage to use even a fraction of 1% more than the 10% most people use, that puts you ahead of the rest.

# How the Sleeping Giant Can Help You

Sit back and think for a minute what it would be like to have the sleeping giant helping you.

Remember, this is the giant who invented things for Tesla, who wrote Mozart's symphonies, who figured out the structure of the benzine molecule. This giant is *heavy artillery*.

Will *your* sleeping giant help you do all these things? Well ... yes and no.

You must have noticed by now that the sleeping giant tends to stick to just one thing. Howe only invented the sewing machine — he didn't start to write music. Mozart only wrote music — he didn't mess about with chemistry.

The other thing about the sleeping giant is that it's a sleeping *giant* not a sleeping wizard. It can't feed you information you don't already have or make you skilled in some area you've never tackled before.

By which I mean, the sleeping giant could play symphonies inside Mozart's head, but if Mozart hadn't known how to write music, that's where it would have stopped.

What's happening here is that the sleeping giant follows a particular person's *interest*.

Tesla, for instance, was interested in electricity, so his sleeping giant fed him electrical ideas and inventions. All Mozart ever wanted to do was write music, so that's all his sleeping giant helped him to do.

But if you're interested in a lot of different things, your sleeping giant can turn its hand to anything.

What interests you?

Maybe you play the guitar. Your sleeping giant will help you play it better.

Maybe you write poetry. Your sleeping giant will feed you inspiration.

Maybe you are having trouble at school. Your sleeping giant will make it easier for you to learn.

Maybe you want to do better at sports. Your sleeping giant will help you do better at sports.

Maybe you want to be more popular. Your sleeping giant will help turn you into the sort of person who's more popular.

Whatever it is you want to do, your sleeping giant will help you do it better and with far less effort.

Let's get specific about this.

Suppose you had three rotten school reports in a row and your parents were threatening you if you collected another one.

You could call in your sleeping giant to help you with some (or all) of the tougher lessons.

You could ask for an improvement of memory or an improvement of understanding or even an improvement of *performance*.

Or forget school altogether. Suppose you're interested in the theatre and have joined your local drama group. They're doing *Hamlet* and you've been cast in a supporting role.

Because you want to make the best possible impression, you could call in the sleeping giant to help you learn your lines.

And help you understand the character better.

And help you get over your stage fright.

And help you project your voice more strongly.

And help you act the part with subtlety.

And give you the confidence to ask for the lead next time.

That sounds little short of miraculous, but when you're dealing with the sleeping giant, miracles of this type really can happen.

One more example. You've just formed a pop group (in which you play drums, to the delight of parents and neighbours on practice nights).

You're realistic. You know every pop group doesn't get into the big time, but some *do* get lucky and you'd like to give it your best shot.

Obviously you could call in the sleeping giant to help you play drums a little more proficiently. But why stop there? The sleeping giant could also help you compose some original numbers for the group, help you achieve the best balance of sound, help you improve your presentation, suggest a few novelties for the act, even dream up a really catchy name for the group.

I go back to what I said at the very beginning. What is it you really want? Because whatever it is, you'll improve your chances of getting it if you chat up your sleeping giant.

But whatever about people like Tesla who seemed to manage it at will, it's not all that easy to chat up your sleeping giant.

On your average waking day, there is a very strong barrier between the giant and you. There has to be, otherwise you couldn't function.

Remember, the sleeping giant is actually your own unconscious mind, the part of you that sends you dreams at night. If there was no barrier, you'd run the risk of dreaming while you're wide awake, thus dramatically increasing your chances of walking under a bus.

But three times a 24-hour day, that barrier comes down.

# How to Usethe Dreaming Giant

The first time the barrier comes down is when you're asleep.

Even though you do it (hopefully without too much difficulty) every night, sleep is not the simple thing you might imagine.

If you bought an electroencephalograph today and plugged it into your head tonight, you would find you actually pass through four totally different *stages* of sleep.

In Stage One sleep, your brain waves speed up and become irregular. This stage only lasts a few minutes. From the inside it feels like you are drifting on the edge of sleep, not quite awake, not quite unconscious either, watching a few woolly visual thoughts float by.

Stage Two sleep starts out with short bursts of rapid, high-peak brain waves that gradually build up into a spindle pattern on the graph. You've stopped drifting and are properly asleep by now. Certainly you won't wake up just because of some light sound or minor disturbance.

The next change in the graph, announcing Stage Three sleep, shows the first appearance of large slow brain waves each one lasting about a second. Anybody trying to wake you up now would have to call your name two or three times, maybe even give you a little shake.

By now your muscles will have relaxed totally, your pulse will have slowed and your temperature dropped.

Eventually those occasional large slow brain waves will become so frequent that they take over the whole chart. When this happens, you are into Stage Four sleep, the deepest sleep there is.

Anybody trying to wake you now will have his work cut out. Only a very loud noise or a vigorous shaking is likely to pull you up from these depths.

Stage Four sleep also last longer than the other three stages, often going on for a couple of hours.

When you first hear about the four stages of sleep, it's very easy to imagine your night as a steady progression from Stage One to Stage Four, then back again as you wake up. But in fact this doesn't happen.

What happens is you hit Stage Four (deep) sleep very early in the night, stay there for an hour and a half, maybe two hours, then race back up very quickly to Stage One.

Only now it is a different sort of Stage One.

In this new, different, Stage One sleep, your body is like a rag doll and it is much tougher to wake you up than it was before. Your eyes have started to flicker from side to side as if you were watching a speeded-up tennis match.

Scientists, intrigued by this rapid eye movement, actually named this new Stage One sleep after it - REM sleep. REM sleep is when you dream.

Everybody dreams and everybody dreams every night. This is true even though you will not have to ask around many of your friends to find one who says (s)he doesn't dream at all.

The fact is people find it very difficult to remember their dreams. Night after night you go through these fantastic Technicolour® adventures and morning after morning you forget all about most of them.

The very few dreams you *do* remember are nearly always those you have late in the night (or early in the morning, if you prefer) just before waking up. Even then, you will manage to forget all but a handful of these within about a minute of opening your eyes.

Most of the time this doesn't matter. Although your dreams are sent you by the sleeping giant of your unconscious mind, ninety per cent of them are rubbish – the giant babbling about things you did the day before, about stuff that might be worrying you, about situations you hope will come about and so on.

This material can be interesting. It's often very entertaining. But short of teaching you what sort of person you are, it's not a lot of use.

The trouble is, there are times when the sleeping giant does send you very important messages indeed through dreams. You've already seen this in the story of how the sewing machine got to be invented and how Kekulé dreamed the structure of benzine.

When a message is important, the sleeping giant can go to a lot of trouble to make sure you pay attention and remember.

Another trick the sleeping giant uses to attract your attention to an important dream is repetition. Dreams which recur over a period of weeks, months or even years, usually have something important to say to you, although it's not always easy to figure out exactly what.

But despite the giant's ability to make dreams dramatic and repeat them often, the message does not always get through.

You probably already know the poem *Kublai Khan* which begins

*In Xanadu did Kublai Khan*
*A stately pleasure dome decree*
*Where Alph the sacred river ran*
*Through caverns measureless to man*
*Down to a sunless sea ...*

What you may not know is that it is unfinished. And the

reason it is unfinished is that Coleridge was interrupted while he was writing it down.

You would imagine any poet worth his salt would have taken up where he left off once his visitor departed. But in this instance, *Kublai Khan* was actually composed by the sleeping giant and presented to Coleridge in a dream. He managed to get some of it written down, but by the time his visitor left, he could not remember the rest.

It makes you wonder how much more important material has been lost because people simply forget their dreams and consequently forget most of the routine messages the sleeping giant sends them.

Fortunately there is something you can do about this. You can record your dreams.

The technique of dream recording is very simple and very difficult. You leave a notepad and pencil within reach of your bed and promise yourself that you will write down every detail you remember of your dreams *the minute you wake up.*

It's that promise that makes it difficult. The minute you

wake up tomorrow morning, you will realise the last thing you want to do is write down your dreams. What you want to do is fall asleep again, or snuggle under the blankets and listen to the rain, or pretend you haven't really woken up and don't have to go to school.

But if you *don't* write your dreams down *at once* you will not be able to write them down at all. They fade away like mist under a morning sun, faster than you would ever have believed possible.

There is one small consolation. Providing you can find the enormous willpower to get started and keep going for a week or two, the morning will come when recording your dreams will be a *habit*.. After that it gets easy.

You will also find – and I know because I've spent a lot of time recording dreams – that once you begin making the effort to record them, you tend to remember more of your dreams and to remember them longer.

Once you start recording your dreams in the mornings, your sleeping giant, who may be big, but isn't stupid, will start putting any important messages into the dreams you do record.

All the same, if you're prepared to make the effort, it is possible to communicate quite well with the sleeping giant while you're fast asleep. And the good news is you can do so with far less effort than you have to put into recording dreams.

The technique is simply to ignore the advice of all the experts and *take your problems to bed with you.*

Taking your problems to bed with you is supposed to be the best way to lose sleep and worry yourself into an early grave. But if you handle it the right way, you'll not only sleep soundly, live long and prosper, but worry far less because most of your problems will be solved by your sleeping giant.

This is the mindpower technique I've used far more than any other and now it works so well it's almost frightening.

What you do is select one (only one) thing that's troubling you and *think about it just before you fall asleep*. Don't try to solve the problem. Don't let it hassle you. Just think about it.

That's all there is to it. Seven times out of ten you'll

wake up next morning with a solution in your head. If you don't, just bring the same problem to bed with you next night (and the night after that, if necessary) until the sleeping giant cracks it.

I use it to write books, because that's what I do for a living. When I finish a day's writing stint, I usually have no idea at all how the book should continue. But that night in bed I think quietly about the last thing I've written and next morning I wake up with the structure of the next chapter in my head – all I have to do is write it down.

It doesn't have to be books. A colleague of mine uses this method to solve mathmatical problems. (That being *his* job.) Another, who's a fashion buyer, finds it helps her decide which lines to stock.

The technique will not work every time, but it will work often enough to be very useful indeed. Remember, if it fails the first night, it is always worth taking the same problem to bed the next night and the next. But only one problem at a time. If you try to solve a bunch of problems this way, your giant only gets confused.

# Your Colour Countdown for Complete Control

The second time the barrier between the sleeping giant and yourself lowers of its own accord is just after you wake up in the morning. The third time is just before you fall asleep at night.

On both occasions, you're in what the experts call a hypnogogic state.

You can recognise the state quite easily. You feel pleasantly drifty and dreamy and relaxed. You're not quite asleep, but you're not fully awake either. It is so close to Stage One sleep I'm not sure there is very much difference between them.

You can use the hypnogogic state to talk directly to your old friend the sleeping giant, but it has its drawbacks. The main one is it's hard to hold. You nearly always slip one way or the other. Either you fall asleep and lose control of your communication, or you wake up and the barrier slams down like a portcullis, cutting it off altogether.

Fortunately, you're not stuck with the two examples of the hypnogogic state that occur naturally. You can actually create your own portable hypnogogic state (or something very like it) at any time of the day.

The first step is physical and mental relaxation.

Some people relax easily, some people don't. Generally speaking, the older you are, the harder it gets. You're not so old, so it shouldn't be too difficult. Try it now. Sit in a chair or lie on the floor and flop. Now lift an arm or a leg (or even a finger) and if it feels really heavy, you're relaxed.

(If you're *not* relaxed and *can't* relax, I've put a full-scale relaxation technique in an Appendix to this book. It's well worth doing regularly until you get the hang of flopping at will.)

But relaxation is only the first step. Your next step is something called a *colour countdown*. It's kind of weird and a lot of fun. Don't be put off by the fact it takes me pages to describe it. When you've actually *done* it a few times, you'll be able to run through the whole sequence in under five minutes.

Here's what you do:

Go somewhere where you won't be disturbed, lie down and make yourself as comfortable as possible.

Where you lie down is up to you. A good cozy bed would be nice, or a couch, but if you can't find these, lie on the floor or snuggle into an easy chair. The important thing is to make yourself really comfortable.

Make sure you're warm enough, kick off your shoes and loosen any tight clothing. Now take yourself through the following sequence:

Relax, close your eyes and take a number of deep, even breaths. (This is NOT the 2/4 breathing of the relaxation technique in the Appendix. It's simply several good, deep, slow breaths.)

As you continue to breathe deeply and easily, imagine yourself standing in the main hallway on the seventh floor of a plush new office building.

This is your office, your building, your company, so

you have every right to be here. Take a little time to look around. You'll notice at once this floor is wholly decorated in red.

The walls have been painted a vivid, warm red. The carpet beneath your feet is red. The ceiling above your head is red. Even the furnishings are a matching red. The effect is quite striking, if a little overpowering.

As you look around you, imagine a large figure 7 standing out against the red walls of this seventh floor.

Walk down the hall until you reach the door to your private elevator at the end. Press the down button at the side and the door slides open at once.

Like everything else on the seventh floor, your private elevator is coloured red — walls, ceiling and carpet on the floor. Even the light inside is a muted red, like a photographer's darkroom lamp only a little brighter.

Step into the elevator, turn to face front, then press the single control button in the wall to your right. The door closes very smoothly and silently and with not so much as a hint of a jolt, you feel yourself beginning to descend.

This is one of the best elevators you have ever been in. Very high-tec, whisper quiet and totally safe. You feel really comfortable, really secure.

And even though you were relaxed to begin with, you now find yourself relaxing even further because you're in your own place and you have complete control here.

As the elevator moves smoothly downwards, take a deep breath then, as you breathe out, repeat the word 'seven' out loud seven times.

Allow the colour red to soak through you as if you were descending through a sea of red. But as you descend, the colour of the light above your head changes very, very slowly from red to a bright orange.

The walls of the elevator are changing colour too, again to bright orange. Even the carpet beneath your feet is turning into an orange carpet. From this change you know you must be approaching the sixth floor.

The elevator glides smoothly to a stop, the door opens and you step out onto the sixth floor which, sure enough, is totally decorated in a bright orange hue.
Here you can see a large figure 6 standing out against

the orange walls.

You walk along this floor, surrounded by the colour orange, until you reach the next down elevator. Once again you step inside, still surrounded by the colour orange. Once again the doors close silently and you begin to glide downwards.

As you begin to move, repeat the word 'six' aloud six times. Feel yourself relaxing even more as the elevator drops gently downwards and notice that you are still totally surrounded by the colour orange.

Eventually, as happened before, the light above your head begins gradually to change, turning from orange to a pleasing golden-yellow.

Once more the walls and floor of the elevator change too to match the light and you know you are approaching the fifth floor.

Sure enough, when the elevator stops and the door opens, you can see the figure 5 prominently printed on the golden-yellow walls of this floor.

Leave the elevator and walk along the yellow corridor

to the next down elevator. This one, as you would expect, is decorated entirely in yellow, with a yellow light set into the ceiling.

Get in and as the door closes, take a deep breath and repeat the word 'five' five times out loud, all the time surrounded by the vivid golden-yellow colour.

You feel extremely comfortable as the elevator glides downwards, very relaxed and very happy.

Eventually, as you continue to descend, the light very gradually changes colour, turning from yellow to a restful, relaxing, grassy green. Soon the entire elevator has turned to this rich, green colour and you know you are arriving at the fourth floor.

As the elevator door opens, you step out into a corridor entirely decorated in the same lush green, with the figure 4 prominently painted on the walls.

You walk along through this green fourth floor until you reach the next down elevator which, like the others, has been decorated to match the colouring of the floor.

Thus you step in to a green elevator, take a deep breath

and pronounce the word 'four' aloud four times while surrounded by the restful and relaxing colour green.

Like all the others, the green elevator glides downwards smoothly until, very gradually, the colouring around you begins to change to a calm, peaceful blue and you realise you are approaching the third floor.

When the door opens and you leave the elevator, you are indeed on a third floor in which the entire decor, floor to ceiling, is based on blue, with the figure 3 prominently painted on the blue walls.

But this time, instead of going directly to the down elevator, stop for a moment to remember a scene from nature where you were particularly relaxed by the colour blue. In blue-grey mountains, for example, or beside a blue lake or sea.

Then, imagining this scene, walk along the blue corridor with the figure 3 so prominent on the walls until you reach the next down elevator.

Enter the elevator under the clear blue light, take a deep breath then say the word 'three' aloud three times. Then press the button which allows the door to close and the elevator to carry you downwards in a sea of blue.

As the elevator descends, you enjoy a great sense of harmony and peace.

Slowly, so very slowly, the light and colour in the elevator changes once again to a deep, restful, purple and you know you are approaching the second floor.

The door glides open and you step out into a corridor decorated in rich purple, floor to ceiling, with a plush purple carpet underfoot and the figure 2 clearly painted on the walls.

You walk along to the next -- and last -- down elevator which, as you expect, is purple too, with a purple light in the ceiling.

Step in, feel the colour purple all around you and pronounce the word 'two' twice aloud. Push the button and feel yourself gliding downwards.

By now, you are feeling wholly relaxed, happier and more relaxed even than when you have conducted a really good physical relaxation exercise. Yet relaxed as you are, you remain alert and can see clearly the purple colour around you.

But eventually the colour slowly changes to a luminous, vibrant ultra-violet and you know you have at last reached the first floor.

The elevator door opens and you step out into the main level of your personal office, totally bathed in a bright, modern, yet very restful ultra-violet light. There is a huge notice FIRST FLOOR beside the elevator and the figure 1 is painted on the walls.

Take a deep breath now and as you exhale, say the word 'one' out loud. You feel very good to have reached your main level, very happy, very secure and very, very relaxed.

Looking around you can see you are not in a corridor, but rather in an ultra-violet hall. Walk across the hall to a door which is prominently marked CONTROL CENTRE.

This door is closed and locked, but when you press your thumb firmly on a small metal plate set in the door about level with your waist, it opens at once with a muted chime.

You walk in to your personal Control Centre, a split-level chamber which reminds you of the bridge of a starship. The light here is still that brilliant, restful ultra-violet and all around you are banks of complex computer controls.

Directly facing the door is an enormous dark viewing screen. Immediately in front of it is an impressive swivel chair, precisely constructed to the dimensions of your body.

Beside the chair, within easy reach, is a control panel which incorporates a microphone intercom. A tiny metal plate is set into the panel near the intercom, like a manufacturer's nameplate. On the plate are engraved two words:

### Sleeping Giant

On this, your first trip to your personal Control Centre, you should positively avoid touching anything in the control room. Take another quick glance around, then return to the main hall, allowing the door to the control room to close and lock behind you.
In the main hall, close your eyes, count slowly from 1 to 3.

On the count of three, leave the imaginary office, and open your eyes on your own room. You will find you feel very refreshed, very relaxed, very alert, calm and happy; maybe even a little bit excited by what you've just experienced.

But believe me, you ain't seen nothing yet!

# How to Wake the Sleeping Giant

If you've followed the instructions in the last chapter, performed the colour countdown and visualised your personal Control Centre, you should congratulate yourself on achieving something very important indeed.

What you have done is built a sophisticated, flexible piece of communications equipment, at least as complicated as a telephone or radio transciever.

It is not a piece of physical equipment – you can't trip over it or kick it – but it is just as real as the house you live in or the bus you take to school.

The equipment is for talking to your sleeping giant, for telling your sleeping giant what you want so you can start to get things moving your way for a change.

You've already done the really hard part by creating the equipment. In this chapter you'll learn how to use it.

Go to your personal Control Centre exactly as you did in the last chapter.

This time, however, walk directly to that swivel chair that looks as if it was made for you. Sit in it and have a look at the screen and the control panel in front of it.

To make your life a little easier, I've included a diagram of the set-up on page ??. As you can see, the viewing screen is in landscape format — that is, it's a lot wider than it is high.

What mightn't be quite so obvious from the diagram is the fact that the screen is curved. It wraps around so you might think it would give a semi 3D effect if you happened to show pictures on it ... and you would be right.

But there are no pictures on the screen right now. It's dark and the only thing you can see on its glassy surface is the odd reflection.

Now take a closer look at the control panel. Right in the middle are two rectangular touchplate switches, one overprinted with the word ON, the other with the word OFF. Above them is the word Mains.

Below these switches, set into the panel itself is the highly sensitive microphone, just above the little metal plaque that says Sleeping Giant.

To the left is the intercom speaker grille. To the right are two more touchplate switches, larger than the others, respectively overprinted with the words SCREEN ON and SCREEN OFF. Immediately below them, underneath the word MIKE are two more touchplates, labelled ON and OFF.

None of that's too complicated, but since it's your first time in, I want you to take it slow and easy. The first step, obviously, is to switch on your communications system at the mains.

Reach out and touch the top of the middle two switches. This is very advanced stuff, because you don't have to press or click or anything like that: just a gentle touch will do.

As you make contact, the switch itself lights up and you can hear a faint hum as the various computers in the Control Centre spring into life. You may also notice just the faintest crackle of static from the speaking grille of the intercom.

The communications system you have set up is now ready to go into operation.

What you do now — and each time you want to make contact with your sleeping giant — is to imagine yourself first reaching out and gently pressing the 'Mike ON' touchplate on your right. As you do so, imagine it begins to glow.

If you tap the mike, the sound will boom out through the entire Control Centre. Try this once and imagine the result.

Now imagine yourself saying very calmly and clearly, 'Calling the Sleeping Giant. Come in, please, Sleeping Giant.'

Got that? 'Calling the Sleeping Giant. Come in, please, Sleeping Giant.'

And imagine that, with only the barest hesitation, a soft voice answers through the intercom panel with the one word, 'Listening ...'

With this sequence, you have established contact. The communication system has been activated and the lines are open. Now all you have to do is send a message.

You do this by reaching out again in your imagination and pressing the touchplate marked SCREEN ON.

As you do so, imagine the touchplate lighting up, followed almost instantly, by the main screen. Look up at that screen and see it glowing with a soft, white light.

This is your active communication screen, the screen on which you will place the pictures you want to send the sleeping giant. This is the real secret of talking to the giant. Because *the sleeping giant thinks in pictures*.

You may actually have noticed this before, without really stopping to figure out what it meant. It's the reason why telling yourself to cheer up never works, but imagining something nice will often do the trick.

Your Control Centre is just a more effective way of doing the same thing. It is a place you have created inside your head where you can send picture messages to the giant direct, while you are in the sort of relaxed state of mind that guarantees the message will get through.

All you have to do is think a picture onto the screen. You should take a little time to play about with this before you start to send the messages for real. Visualise a single item — like a bowl of flowers — and imagine it appearing on the screen.

Now try a more complicated picture, like a parkland scene with trees and a lake and a couple of old age pensioners feeding the ducks out of brown paper bags. Watch that come up on the screen as well.

Take as much time as you need to get the feel of using your imagination this way. You can, of course, make more than one visit to your personal Control Centre in order to get used to it.

Once you've got the feel of using the controls and thinking pictures onto the screen, you can send your first message. Remember, you're not just saying *Hi*. The sleeping giant is there to help you.

And to show just how powerful, how far-reaching this help can be, I'd suggest you go for broke and ask the sleeping giant to make you feel a whole lot better about yourself.

Remember your P3, your Personal Potential Percentage, and how it wasn't high enough? Ask the sleeping giant to give your P3 a boost. That way, you'll not only feel good, but you can actually *measure the improvement* by taking the test again and comparing the latest results to what you got originally.

Here's how you can go about it:

Visit your Control Centre, switch on as you've just done now, make contact with the Sleeping Giant, then use the big view-screen to see yourself *as you would like yourself to be*.

If you think of yourself as a nervous type, imagine yourself going about things calmly.

If you think of yourself as pretty dim, visualise yourself zipping through your schoolwork like a genius.

If you think you're ugly, imagine yourself handsome or beautiful.

I don't know what it is you need, but you do. Make the pictures on your inner screen as vivid, active and detailed as possible. Don't settle for a flickery black and white old silent movie like something Charlie Chaplin would have starred in. What you're after is a full-scale Technicolour® production with a cast of thousands and quadraphonic sound.

Start each scene from the outside. That is, see yourself up there on the screen as if you were watching a movie you had actually made. See the way you look, the way you move, the way you dress. Hear the way you talk. Note your personal mannerisms.

And don't lose sight of the fact that you're imagining yourself as you wish to be so it's quite all right if you're bigger, smarter, smoother, tougher, better-looking, charming or whatever.

But however many positive changes you make in yourself, be sure the scenes themselves are realistic. Watch yourself in everyday situations, facing everyday problems ... and dealing with your life better than you ever did before.

Watch how other people — the people you know — react to you. And remember, since you're the producer of this movie, you can control what the other actors do just as much as you control what you do yourself.

Let's take a concrete example. Suppose you're worried about your popularity, as most people are. Suppose that normally you go to parties or to discos and skulk in dark corners because you're hassled people don't really like you all that much.

In a situation like this, you should visualise a party on the screen. You should see it in full swing. You should imagine all the people who are important to you at that party.

But instead of imagining yourself skulking in a corner as would be the case in real life, see yourself walking into that party very relaxed, very confident. *And imagine everybody in the place delighted to see you.*

You can ham it up a little if you like. Have them stop the music and applaud when you walk in. Have them crowd around you, anxious to talk to you, anxious to have you notice them.

Once you have run through a scene from the outside, move on to the second stage. Project yourself *into* the screen and imagine how the scene continues from the inside.

At this point, you should put effort into making the whole thing as realistic and vivid as possible. Try to smell scents, feel textures, hear sounds as well as see the action. Try to imagine yourself as if you were really there.

And all the time imagine yourself as you wish to be, doing what you want to do, succeeding as you want to succeed, creating the impression you want to create.

If you're like most people, you'll enjoy this technique. But don't underestimate it because of that. The interesting thing about the example I've just given is that even though it should theoretically only make you feel a bit less worried about your popularity, what it will actually do is *increase* your popularity.

This is because your mental pictures told the sleeping giant what it was you wanted to be. So the sleeping giant starts making subtle adjustmnents in your attitudes so that you *become* more popular.

Of course, that sort of result doesn't happen all at once. It may take weeks, maybe even months to achieve. And it will probably take more than one session in your Control Centre.

But if you repeat the exercise once a day, spending no more than a few minutes on each session, you'll get there.

When you've finished each session, come out of your Control Centre into the main ultra-violet level and do the three count to get back to normal exactly as you did earlier earlier.

At the end of about three weeks visualising yourself as you would like to be, take a day off and do that Personal Potential test again.

When you work it through, I'm willing to bet your P3 score has improved. If I'm right, then you've just proved how effective your contact with the sleeping giant can be.

# The Magic of Music

Now you've improved your Personal Potential Percentage, you might figure you've got a good grip on the sleeping giant ... and you would be right.

In fact, you could go on the Control Centre exactly as before and still get excellent results.

But you can do even better.

At the risk of frightening you to death, I have to tell you what you've been doing is properly called autogenic training.

Much of the recent scientific work on autogenic training was done in the USSR where they discovered something very odd.

It all works better if you do it to music.

But not just any music. What does the trick is parts — and only parts — of a special type of classical music called baroque.

Baroque music goes back to the days of Johann Sebastian Bach who at one stage of his career was called in by the Russian Envoy, Count Kayserling, to help with a serious problem.

Kayserling had difficulty sleeping.

Somehow, Kayserling got it into his head that a little light music might help. So he called in Bach and asked him to compose something bright and interesting, but calm.

Kayserling was right. Only minutes after hearing Bach's specially composed music, he felt the tensions beginning to drain from his body. Soon he was fast asleep, allowing Goldberg to creep away to his own warm bed.

From then on, Kayserling slept a great deal better than Goldberg, who was hired to sit up with his harpsichord in the room next to the Count's bedroom in case he was required to play Bach's special sleep music again. Each time he did so, Kayserling dozed off promptly.

The music that did the trick is now known as the Goldberg Variations after the obliging harpsichordist. Bach himself received a substantial sum of money for composing it.

This may sound like a very long-winded way of saying music helps you relax, but it isn't. Relaxation, it turns out, is only part of the picture. What seems to be happening is that a certain *type* of music (and *only* that type of music) has a weird effect on the human mind. It certainly helps you relax, but it does something else as well.

But if you're not interested in sleeping (and not over tired to begin with) this special sort of music does something totally different. It helps you visualise more clearly.

Not every bit of music written will do the trick. Lozanov's investigation actually concentrated on the largo (slow) movements of their concertos.

But whatever the reason, your Control Centre will work better if you set it to this special music. The result has nothing to do with your personal taste. Like it or loathe it, the music still works.

There's a list of suitable pieces in Appendix 2 which you can use as a guide if you want to put together your own background music programme. Most record shops have a classical music section, so you can listen to a few samples next time you're in to buy U2.

Alternatively, you can see what you can find in the works of any baroque composer.

Keep away from vocals or chants, even if they have the right tempo -- they're too distracting. String instruments seem to give best results, so favour these if you have a choice.

Your aim is to put together a programme which runs for the length of your relaxation and visualisation sessions, so you don't really need all that much.

If you happen to be able to play an instrument yourself — especially a string instrument like a violin or guitar — there's nothing to stop you recording your own baroque variations. Just make sure the tempo is at, or very close to, 60 beats per minute and you should get the results you want.

Once you have your special music programme together,

using it is straightforward. Switch on as you begin your colour countdown. Allow the music to run for a moment or two before you imagine yourself on the seventh floor, then run it right through until you have finished in the Control Centre.

# How the Sleeping Giant Can Help You Do the Impossible

What you've really done with the techniques you've learned so far is to bring a part of your own mind under control.

It sounds a simple enough thing put like that. But once you've done it, you can start to achieve things that simply wouldn't have been possible before.

Years ago I wrote a book called *Getting What You Want*, which was about the use of mindpower (and some other sneakier techniques) in business situations.

The first thing I told readers of that book was a four-word secret designed to help them get ahead not just in business, but in any aspect of their lives. What I told them was this:

*Your limitations are imaginary.*

You wouldn't want to take that too literally. Obviously you are stuck with some limitations. Try lifting a ton weight with one hand, for example.

But I believed then and I believe now that the important limitations, the limitations which stop you doing the things you really want to do, are all imaginary.

That needs a little explanation. I'm not trying to tell you that your limitations don't exist.. You wouldn't believe me if I did. What I'm telling you is that they only exist inside your head.

Here's an example:

You know that running a mile in four minutes is difficult. But up to May 1954, it wasn't just difficult — it was downright impossible.

A hundred years before that date, the best mile time anybody in the world could manage was around five minutes. In 1861, an Irishman named Heaviside set a record at 4 minutes 55 seconds.

Of course, records are made to be broken. In the years that followed, athletes nibbled bits off it, bringing it down two, three, even four seconds at a time. Just as the Second World War was ending, a Swede called Gunder Hägg got it all the way to 4 minutes 1.3 seconds.

You'd imagine it shouldn't have been too hard to shave off that final 1.3 seconds and run a four-minute mile. But for nine years, runner after runner tried ... and failed.

These were the world's top athletes, fit, highly trained and motivated men from Britain, America, Europe. Every one knew that the first man to run a sub four-minute mile would be world famous within hours and into the sporting history books forever.

And still not one could manage it.

This did not come as a surprise to certain members of the medical profession. They thought four minutes for the mile marked the outer limit of human endurance.

On the face of it, this was not a dumb idea. After all, you can't keep running faster and faster all the time. There has to come a stage where, no matter how fit and well trained you are, you're up against what is actually possible for your body.

When it comes to running, the human body is a machine. And its basic design limits the sort of speed it can get up to. In 1954, many doctors, trainers and athletes believed a 4-minute mile was definitely the limit.

There were, however, a few people who didn't believe it. One was a 25-year-old medical student called Roger Bannister.

Bannister figured a sub four-minute mile might be tough, but it wasn't actually impossible. He was certain that he could run a mile somewhere around 3 minutes 59 seconds and still manage to survive.

He put this conviction to the test on a number of occasions, without, however, breaking the four-minute barrier.

Then came the athletics match between Oxford University and the Amateur Athletics Association at Iffley Road on May 6, 1954.

Worried that overseas athletes might beat him to the record, Bannister had determined on another attempt, aided by his friends Chris Chataway and Chris Brasher. who had both agreed to act as pacemakers.

Although there was a high, cold wind to contend with, Bannister ran the final lap in 59 seconds and the overall mile in 3 minutes 59.4 seconds.

He collapsed exhausted as he crossed the line, but his heart had not burst and when he got up again, no bits fell off his body. Deservedly, he lived to enjoy the world-wide recognition that followed his achievement.

But that's not the interesting bit. The interesting bit is that inside a few weeks of Bannister's historic run, the four minute barrier was broken again ... and again ... and again.

Today, of course, sub four minute miles are commonplace at top international track events. Training methods and even the standard of the tracks themselves have all improved, helping athletes towards better times.

But how do we explain the sudden rush of four-minute milers so quickly after Bannister broke the barrier? At that time, the training methods were the same and the tracks were the same.

The answer is simple. Bannister had proved it could be done. The four minute barrier was not, as it happened, the limit of human endurance. The barrier existed only in the minds of those who believed in it.

It was, in other words, an imaginary limitation.

In fact, the four-minute mile was a classic example of an imaginary limitation — and one that achieved worldwide proportions. But there have been others.

If something is impossible, you definitely can't do it. If something isn't, there's a chance you can.

Let's bring all this home. Collect up your pen and paper one more time and head off for that famous room where you won't be disturbed. Sit down and make a list of everything you'd like to do, but know to be impossible.

Maybe you'd like to be Head Boy or Head Girl at your school, but you know you'd never manage that.

Maybe you fancy becoming a world famous pop star, but you know you never will.

Maybe you just want to be a billionaire, but you know that's quite impossible.

Maybe your list won't include any of these things. It's your list . You're the one who knows what you want and what's impossible for you.

When you've finished writing, read it over. Because nine times out of ten, ninety-nine times out of a hundred, the sleeping giant can help you achieve those things you listed as impossible.

And in our very next section, you'll start to find out how.

# Getting Your Self-Image into Shape

If you've worked through this book from the beginning, your self image will already be improved by now — and the results shown up on your latest P3.

But you can do better. In fact, you can do a whole lot better.

Start by thinking about yourself. Make a rigorous, honest self-examination.

You should look at yourself, your attitudes, habits, even your appearance, with special emphasis on any aspect of yourself you feel to be negative or limiting to what you want to do.

In particular, try to figure out how other people really see you.

Be careful about this. We're not talking about how you *think* other people see you — that's what the Personal

Potential Test was for.

And we're not talking about how you would *like* them to see you — you went that route when you worked on your self image in the Control Room.

What you're after, as coolly as you can manage, without fooling yourself in any way, is how others *really* see you. If you find this difficult, a good approach is to try to imagine how you would see you if you were somebody else.

Write down (in note form) everything you realise about yourself.

Before your next mindpower session, read over your notes to refresh your mind, then, using your colour countdown as before, go to your Control Centre.

Open up communication with the sleeping giant, then switch on the view screen.

What you're going to do now is rework those negative aspects of your character that you've discovered. Since I don't know what they are, I can't tell you exactly how to do this, but I can give you a couple of examples of the technique.

Let's suppose one of the things you learned about yourself was that you feel afraid a lot of the time.

Fear is something everybody feels, of course, but you may have decided you are a fearful individual and want to do something about it.

The first step is to recognise that however fearful you are, however often you feel fear, you definitely are not fearful *all the time*. Your fear arises *in response to certain situations.*

Maybe you're afraid of your teachers at school. Maybe you're afraid of speaking in public. Maybe you're afraid when you take part in sports.

What you're looking for are the situations in which you *most often* feel afraid.

Take three or four of these situations and throw them up on the screen. See the situation that makes you afraid and watch yourself being afraid in it.

Don't spend too long over this, but do try to make the

visualisation as vivid as you can. Try to feel the fear the situation usually calls up in you.

When you have done that, hit the SCREEN OFF touchplate.

Pressing this button wipes the picture from the screen; and at the same time you should put it, and the fear, out of your mind. Imagine the whole inside of your head and body has been washed clean of the situation and the fear.

Once you've done that, press the SCREEN ON touchplate so the screen lights up again. Now use the screen to imagine you are back in the same situation *except this time you do not react to it with fear.* Imagine yourself dealing with it coolly and calmly.

When you have done that, imagine the whole scene spinning into a tight little ball and draw the ball inside yourself before switching off the screen.

This is a technique that you can use for just about any negative aspect of your character, not just fear.

Maybe you're worried that you're too aggressive. Set

up the screen to show you how you act and react in aggressive situations. Watch how your aggression affects other people. Then wipe the screen using the SCREEN OFF plate, switch on again and relive the situation without aggression.

Maybe you're worried about lack of concentration. Set up the screen to show how you bumble through a situation hardly knowing what time of day it is. Switch off to clear the picture from your mind, then switch on again and rework the scene imagining yourself concentrating like a laser.

If every case, roll the second scene — the one where you're doing it the way you want to — into a ball and draw it out of the screen into yourself.

Let's recap the technique.

1. First, figure out what negative aspects of your personality you wish to change.

2. Go into your Control Room.

3. View on screen typical situations in which your negative aspects show themselves.

4. Use the SCREEN OFF switch to clear them from your mind.

5. View on screen those same situations changed so that you are now acting in a positive way.

6. Roll up the positive scenes and draw them into yourself.

Once again, it may take a few sessions. You didn't build up your bad habits in a day, so don't expect to break them down at one shot either. But stick at it and you'll soon find you have banished a whole heap of things about yourself that hassled you – negative thoughts, fears, bad reactions – and banished them for good.

# How to Hire
# the Sleeping Giant
# as Your Sports Coach

It's useful to have the sleeping giant on your side whatever you're doing, but results are specially impressive — and show particularly quickly — in sports.

Before you use mindpower, however, you need to use a bit of brainpower and try to figure out what makes for successful sporting performance.

Of course there are sports and sports. And what makes you good at clay-pigeon shooting wouldn't necessarily turn you into a world-class weight-lifter.

All the same, when you get right down to it, there are some elements you'll find in all sports:

* Enthusiasm

* Energy

* Good health

* Technique

* Strategy

* Self discipline

And there are additional elements you'll find in some sports:

* Strength

* Agility

* Teamwork

* Endurance

The good news is the sleeping giant can help you in every one of these areas. Let's take them in order.

**Enthusiasm**

The theory is you wouldn't be taking part in a particular

sport unless you were already enthusiastic about it.

The reality is that your motivations for playing don't have to include enthusiasm at all. You might, for example, go to a school where games are actually compulsory, so you're actually forced to roll about in the mud once a week.

Or you might have taken up a particular sport to please your parents or impress your friends. Or you might be doing it under medical orders or because you decided it was the best way to get fit.

You might even be doing it to avoid doing something even worse.

These are all perfectly legitimate reasons for engaging in sports and none of them involve even the slightest degree of enthusiasm.

But if you want to be good at a particular sport, enthusiasm would help. And even if you don't, enthusiasm would certainly make the whole thing far more pleasant.

To generate enthusiasm (which bubbles up from your

unconscious mind like fizz from *7-Up* ) use the colour countdown to reach your Control Centre, then spend the next fifteen or twenty minutes thinking about your chosen sport. Specifically, think about those aspects of your chosen sport you really do enjoy.

I appreciate this might be difficult. I was forced to play rugby once a week in season for six years and hated every minute of it. But that was before I discovered mindpower. Now I know that if you dig deep enough there's always something you enjoy, even if it's only the hot shower afterwards.

Dig out as many nuggets of enjoyment as you can and make a mental (or physical) note of what they are. Then switch on your viewing screen and put up a picture of the first aspect of your sport that you have decided you enjoy.

Watch yourself taking pleasure in that aspect, but hold the picture so it only deals with the aspect you enjoy. Don't let any other aspect of the sport come in.

Suppose you hate football, but enjoy scoring goals. Put up on screen the movie of you scoring, but don't bother with the moves that led up to the score or anything that happened afterwards. Your mental movie should only be of the score itself.

When you have the scene up there, imagine that it starts to flow like water — a little special effect here — and drains away into a small green capsule.

Imagine you take this capsule and drop it into a neat little box. Then put up the next scene featuring an aspect of the sport you actually enjoy.

Treat this scene exactly as you did the first, watching it turn to liquid and drain into a small green capsule, which you put into the box with the first one.

Keep going, aspect by aspect, until you have worked your way through the list you drew up. Then close down your control panel, lock up the Control Room and leave your level in the usual way.

Now comes the interesting part. Next time you have to play your chosen sport, take a moment in the changing room to close your eyes and imagine yourself swallowing the little green capsules you made up in your Control Centre.

If you only managed to make up one, that's okay. But if you made up more, swallow them all.

Don't make a big deal of this. Close your eyes, do it, then forget it and get on with your game. It should all happen so fast that even if somebody is watching you, all they should see if you squinching up your eyes for a second as if they were a bit tired.

The effect of these imaginary capsules is subtle. You won't suddenly be changed into a raging enthusiast the way Dr Banner turns into the Incredible Hulk. But afterwards, looking back, you'll find you enjoyed that game far more than usual.

Keep taking the imaginary capsules before each game and enthusiasm will gradually build up.

**Energy & Good Health**

Since your energy levels are important outside of sport, I've given them a section of their own, so you'll be able to do something about them when you come to them. Fixing your energy will normally help your health as well.

**Technique**

Technique is one of the easiest things to improve by mindpower. But there's a warning:

Before you do anything make sure you know the proper technique for the sport.

Let's suppose you're a tennis buff and want to improve your service. You might be tempted to go to your Control Centre and throw up a mental movie of yourself smashing them down the centre court to the consternation of your opponent.

Which would be fine if the only thing you wanted to improve was your confidence. But could be very tricky if you happened to be visualising your present (utterly hopeless) technique.

So before you make any mindpower move on the technique associated with your sport, take time to study what an expert technique looks like.

Don't mess about with this. Go to the top. Watch television, videos or movies of the world's best players in action. Go and watch them in actual games if possible. Read books on the technique wherever you can find them.

Then, when you are certain you know in theory how it should be done, take yourself off to your Control Centre and put yourself up there on screen using the best possible technique.

Do this, daily if possible, until you see the improvement in your own game. And keep doing it until you have honed your game technique as finely as it will go.

One interesting point. If you find yourself unable to play your chosen game for any reason — illness or injury for example — you can use your Control Centre to keep yourself in practice.

More and more professional sportspeople are using this 'inner game' technique, not because they are particularly interested in mindpower, but simply because they have found it works, allowing them to come back to peak performance after injury far faster than would otherwise have been the case.

## Strategy

Sports strategy is actually a combination of two very different factors — the ability to plan ahead and the ability to think on your feet.

Many an excellent game plan, carefully worked out in the changing rooms, has nosedived on the field because a player or players were unable to modify it to suit prevailing conditions.

But once you recognise the dual aspect of sports strategy, you're off and running. You start by sitting quietly for as long as it takes to work out what you feel to be the best strategy in the circumstances.

Once your strategy is worked out, move into your Control Centre and run it through on screen.

This time, however, you should take care not to visualise everything working perfectly and your strategy carrying you through miraculously to victory. Simply run it in a realistic game setting *and see what happens*.

What you're doing here is that Tesla did when he built a

machine in his imagination and let it run for a few weeks. You're looking for the flaws.

Now the odd thing is, if you're perfectly relaxed and prepared simply to watch the game unfold on your viewscreen, the flaws in your strategy will quickly become obvious — especially if you visualise yourself (or your team) playing against the world's best.

Once the flaws start to show, correct them. Sometimes you can do that right up there on the screen. Other times a more serious flaw in your strategy will come up, forcing you to redraft the whole thing.

Have patience. You can take a long time getting game strategy absolutely right. But when you've ironed out as many bugs as you can find, then you go back to your Control Centre and visualise everything working perfectly and your strategy carrying you through miraculously to victory.

**Self Discipline**

To be perfectly frank, if you have begun to practise mindpower seriously, your self discipline should be very well trained by now without your needing to do anything more about it.

But you know yourself better than I do, so if you think you're slipping a little in the self discipline department, you can give yourself a shot in the arm by visiting your Control Centre and mocking up a series of mental movies showing yourself valiantly struggling on against almost insurmountable hardships and difficulties. It will help.

# Introducing:
# the Advisor Within

Sometimes all the mindpower in the world won't help, because you're faced with a brand new situation and you don't know what to do. Sometimes the only thing that will help is advice.

Sometimes you just need somebody to talk to.

You're not the first to feel that way. One of the greatest living exponents of mindpower is a man named José Silva. Silva was born in Laredo, Texas, in 1914. His family background was poor and got worse when his father died.

By the age of six young José had become the breadwinner doing odd jobs like shining shoes and selling newspapers. It left no time for him to go to school: his brother and sister helped him learn how to read and write.

When he was fifteen years old, Silva went into the radio

repair business. (He'd done a deal with a local barber who subsidised him in a correspondence course on the understanding that Silva would take the exams in the barber's name so the barber would have an impressive certificate to hang up in his shop.)

He prospered in this business, but eventually decided money wasn't everything. The decision was reinforced by his experience of being drafted into the Signal Corps during World War II. He was asked a series of questions by an Army psychiatrist which he considered just about the stupidest he'd ever heard.

But the questions set Silva thinking about the potential of the human mind and started him on a lifelong investigation which moved via hypnosis to mind control and a training system similar in many ways to the exercises you have been using in this book.

Silva developed exercises that raised IQ, improved memory, increased your learning speed and even, so his followers now claim, stimulated wild talents like telepathy.

But it wasn't enough. His course today includes instructions in calling on mental counsellors, people who exist only in your mind, but who can nevertheless give you help and advice.

This sounds really daft when you first come across it, but in fact the idea of the Advisor Within is far older than José Silva.

For centuries, religious contemplatives and mystics of all description have looked inside themselves for wisdom and guidance.

Some, like Silva, developed specific techniques to make such consultations easier.

The technique you can use to contact your own Advisor Within is based on what you have already learned, so you should find it fairly easy.

First, as always, go to your Control Centre.

Once there, you should sit down, relax as deeply as possible and decide whose advice you would value most in all the world.

This can be advice from anybody , male or female, living or dead. You can select a member of your own family, or an old friend, or a teacher, or a television personality, or a world leader, or an ancient philosopher or religious personage.

There are absolutely no limitations on your choice, except that you may pick only one individual.

Take all the time you need to make this decision, because it is important. You may even want to take more than one trip to your Control Centre before you commit yourself finally.

Once the decision is made, gently press the brass plate at the bottom of your control console engraved with the words *Sleeping Giant*.

Pressing this plate activates a special control which lights up the viewing screen without your having to switch it on. As it lights up, a picture will appear on the screen, the picture of a warm, comfortable chamber, furnished with shelves of ancient books on two walls and an old leather armchair drawn up beside a blazing log fire.

The person you have chosen as your Inner Advisor is seated in this armchair. (S)he stands up and moves so that (s)he is looking directly at you from out of the screen.

Visualise this as clearly and vividly as you can. Try to imagine every detail of the face, from the line of the nose to the colour of the eyes.

Thank the Advisor for coming, then ask whatever question, or begin whatever discussion you wish. Try to imagine the replies and advice you would receive from the Advisor.

This may sound as if you're talking to yourself, and in a way you are. But after a while, particularly if you are visualising clearly, something very odd will happen. Your Inner Advisor will begin to take on a life of his/her own.

What you are experiencing here is something very familiar to novelists. They create characters for their books and if they do the job well, the characters actually take control of the story, often refusing point-blank to follow the author's plot or do what he wants them to do.

But whatever makes the Inner Advisor take on a life of

his/her own, the plain fact is it happens. And when it happens, it allows you to gain access to advice and information not usually available to you.

Bear in mind, you don't have to take the advice. The Inner Advisor certainly won't mind if you ignore it.

But very often it helps just to talk things over with a sympathetic listener and get a second opinion on your own decisions. For this, your Inner Advisor will always be there.

# The 9-point Checklist that Turns Desires into Goals and Helps Them Come True

Now you've reached this far, you will certainly have become skilled in the use of mindpower techniques and should have some experience of how effective they can be.

After all that work, you definitely deserve some sort of reward; and if you haven't already sorted out your own rewards through mindpower, then this section is definitely for you.

Right back at the beginning of this book, I asked you what it was you really wanted. Now I'm going to show you how to get it by applying mindpower (relaxation and visualisation) techniques in precisely the right way.

You may recall that when you started out, you made four lists. One was of things you needed right now. One was of things you wanted now or sometime in the future. The third was skills, talents and qualities you needed. The fourth was skills, talents and qualities you wanted.

Find those lists now and prepare to start the work that will vastly increase your chances of turning both your needs and your desires into reality.

You may remember back in Section One I told you that you got ahead of the posse just by making out those lists, since most people never really decide what it is they want. Now you're going to move even further ahead by taking steps to get it.

The first thing you have to do is change your lists into goals. You can do that by checking everything you've written down against this nine-point checklist:

# The 9-point Checklist That Turns Wants into GOALS.

1. Do you really want it?

2. Does it contradict some other goal?

3. Does it produce any problems?

4. Is it positive?

5. Is it detailed?

6. Is it realistic?

7. Is it high enough?

8. Have you included the personality factors needed to achieve it?

9. Is it expressed as if you have already achieved it?

Some of those points require a little explanation.

**1: Do you really want it?**

A lot of people get very mixed up about what they want and don't want. I tried to help you guard against this by telling you to keep your lists private.

Maybe there are one or two things in there that you don't really want at all. Maybe you put something down you thought might please your parents, or your teachers or somebody you want to impress. Go through all four lists again and put your pen through anything you don't really want.

**2: Does it contradict some other goal?**

It's funny how often this one creeps up. You'd think that people would just naturally avoid contradictions, but they don't.

Go through each listed item very carefully, asking yourself each time whether it contradicts some other item on the same list or one of the other lists.

For example, in one place you might have put down

that you want a gold-plated Lamborghini Muira, in another that you want your own castle in Germany, and in a third that you want to earn £15,000 a year.

There's a big contradiction in there. You can't run that sort of car and that sort of pad on that sort of money.

But don't get the idea you have to cross out the car or the castle. What you have to do is raise the amount of money you need to cover them. (I reckon a couple of million should do the trick.)

In each case where you find a contradiction, amend your list to get rid of it.

### 3. Does it produce any problems?

This one can be tricky. Most worthwhile things produce problems sooner or later, but what you're actually looking for here is problems you can't handle.

Nobody lives in a vacuum, so maybe the people you love could get very hassled about some of the things you've listed.

That 500cc motor bike, for example, might be very nice

to have, but could you really handle your folks getting sick with worry every time you took it out?

If you come across examples like that in your lists, you only have two choices. You either take the item off, or try your hand at solving the problem it produces.

The thing is, to be really sure of giving mindpower its best shot, you need to solve the problem before you try to get the item ... and that isn't always too easy.

**4: Is it positive?**

Every potential goal on your four lists should be expressed positively.

If you've written down something like I want to get rid of my asthma, change it round so it becomes a positive statement like, I want to enjoy perfect health.

Most people have a wealth of things they want to get rid of — pains, problems, bad habits, even a relative or two.

But goal lists are all about the things you want, not the things you don't want. If any negative statement has crept into your lists, change it around so you express the same thought positively.

**5: Is it detailed?**

This is the place where nearly everybody falls apart. They're simply not used to the idea they can really go after the things they want, so even when they try to list them, they get very fuzzy in their thinking.

Have you put down on your list that you want a new bike? Nothing wrong with that, except it isn't detailed.

What colour of bike do you want? What make? How many gears? Any special type of wheels? Would you like it hand-made, or would you settle for a factory model?

Go through your lists very carefully with checkpoint No. 5 in mind. In every case, draw up as full a specification for the item you want as if you were ordering it by phone.

This actually could take you quite a time, but the effort will be well worthwhile. People who know what they want tend to get it sooner or later. People who know exactly what they want tend to get it sooner.

## 6: Is it realistic?

I don't want to cramp your style, but we're not in the miracle business here. Run through your lists, item by item, and ask yourself at easy one: Is this realistic?

But don't get swallowed up by imaginary limitations either. Realistic doesn't mean realistic for you. It just means realistic.

For example, you may have put down somewhere that you want a million pounds. Now however you feel about your ability to get your grubby little hands on a million smackeroos, there's nothing unrealistic about that goal.

The acid test for this checkpoint is whether there is somebody, somewhere, who has the thing (or quality) you want. If the answer is yes, then it's not unrealistic.

So it's okay to say you want to fly to Australia in your own private jet plane, because there are people who really do that. It's not okay to say you want to fly to Australia by flapping your arms up and down, because that's just plain unrealistic.

## 7: Is it high enough?

If there is a single thing that stops people getting what they really want, it must be setting their sights too low.

This is a very human failing, because it relates to your level of self-confidence.

Now that you've been using mindpower, your level of self-confidence should have increased very nicely.

But you made those lists before you started using mindpower, so chances are they contain at least some items where you compromised, where you decided there was no chance of getting what you really wanted, so you put down something else you thought you could get.

Now you have to go through those lists again, with your new-found self-confidence, and make sure you're really listing as much as you want of everything you want.

If you really want a skyscraper, don't settle for a bungalow.

## 8: Have you included the personality factors needed to achieve it?

This one is particularly important because it's actually the key that makes the whole system work.

I'll come back to the mechanics of the whole thing in a minute. For now, I just want to say it's pointless putting down you want to run a multi-national corporation with a staff of thousands and an income of billions if you don't also put down that you want energy and discipline and intelligence as well.

Examine every thing you've put down on lists 1 and 2 and try to figure out what talents, characteristics etc you need to get it. Then move over to lists 3 and 4 and make sure the necessary characteristics are included.

## 9: Is it expressed as if you have already achieved it?

I doubt that it is, because I cheated a little and didn't tell you about this one until now.

But as you've probably gathered, you'll soon be presenting these lists to the sleeping giant and the sleeping giant doesn't have too good an idea of time.

This doesn't matter too much when you visualise, because your mind's eye sees things here and now. But there's a verbal element to this system and you want to make sure the sleeping giant understands you want the stuff today, not sometime next year or next century.

So sit down and rewrite your lists so everything in them is expressed as if you already had it.

When you've finished your rewrite, you're ready to roll. This is what you do:

Tell no-one of your goals, your goal lists or your methods.

Each morning immediately after waking:

a) Read your goal lists aloud (if possible) or silently and carefully if not.

b) Use your relaxation and colour countdown to go to your Control Centre. Put each goal up on your viewscreen after making contact with the sleeping giant.

Each evening, before you go to bed, repeat the entire process.

That's it — the whole system. Follow it and I can guarantee you will vastly improve your chances of getting what you want. Here's why.

First, as I mentioned before, only a tiny percentage of people ever actually define their goals. Just defining your goals substantially increases your chances of achieving them.

Next, your limitations are imaginary. Not unreal, but imaginary in the sense that they have been built into your imagination from childhood.

But since imagination put them there in the first place, imagination can be used to break them down.

It is important not to miss a single day. Conditioning is a continuous process. If you miss, you go back to the beginning of the sequence.

Finally, mindpower visualisations put you in touch with your own unconscious mind, the sleeping giant who will aid you in achieving those things you want to achieve.

How long will it take? That varies, depending on your

ability to visualise, your level of self confidence and what it is you wish to achieve.

Some things — and not necessarily the small things — can be achieved quickly. Others can take years.

In general, things that involve changing yourself tend to be fast and fairly easy. When it comes to things that involve the world outside yourself, it can be slow. But if you persevere, you'll get there.

Provided, of course, you know the final secret.

# The Secret of the Final Secret

The secret of the final secret is very simple, very short, very easy to understand, but so important I've decided to give it a section of its own.

The secret's called *opening up the channels*.

What it comes down to is this. However deeply you relax, however vividly you visualise, however clearly you communicate with the sleeping giant, however expertly and skillfully you apply the techniques of mindpower, there's no way you'll get to be Prime Minister if you're stranded on a desert island.

Mindpower isn't magic, however much it seems like magic sometimes. It works through perfectly normal, perfectly everyday channels.

And those channels must be open.

Let's take a brief look at what that means in practice.

Assume one of your goals was to own a new CD player. You've worked out in detail exactly what sort of CD player you want — make, model, colour, the lot.

You've relaxed. You've visualised. And now you're waiting.

But your new CD player isn't going to appear in a puff of purple smoke. It's not going to fall through the ceiling. It won't turn up mysteriously in a locked cabinet.

If you're going to get that new CD at all, you'll get it through normal channels. Which in practical terms means you get it as a gift, as an exchange, or work for it.

Either way, you must make sure to open up the channels.

If you want it as a gift, it's no use hiding in your room and only coming out to be rude to people. Nobody gets gifts that way. Try being pleasant. Try spreading round a few favours. Try doing the washing up, for heaven's sake.

In other words, make yourself the sort of human being people just naturally want to give gifts to. Open up the channel.

You want to be Head Prefect of your school? Use mindpower, but don't forget to put your name forward for election. That's opening up the channel.

You want to own a home computer? Use mindpower and learn electronics so you can build one. That's opening up a channel.

When you think about it, you'll discover there are literally dozens of channels to most of your goals. Use mindpower and open up as many of them as you can.

And by using mindpower you'll soon find you've changed your self image and opened up a long and pleasant road to success.

# APPENDIX 1
## Special Relaxation Exercise

If you have trouble relaxing, try this relaxation sequence. How much time you spend is up to you, but anything less than 10 minutes isn't really worthwhile; and anything above half an hour is too much. But do it regularly. Ten minutes every day for a week is worth more than three hours every now and again.

Conduct your relaxation session in an upright chair. Don't lieon a couch or bed: you'll only fall asleep.

Begin by regulating your breathing.

Your muscles use oxygen extracted from your blood. Your blood extracts that oxygen from the air you breathe. By regulating your breathing, you increase the oxygen in your blood, your muscles extract more and relax better. Here's how to do it:

1. Breathe in to the mental count of four...

2. Hold your breath in to the mental count of two...

3. Breathe out to the mental count of four...

4.  Hold your breath out to the mental count of two.

It sounds simple and it is, although there's a knack to getting it right. (You'll know you've gotten it right when you start to do it without thinking.)

The rate at which you should count varies from person to person. Start by counting along with your heartbeat. If this doesn't work, play around until you hit on a rhythm that's comfortable.

Get your breathing right before you go on to the second part of the exercise.

Once you have established a comfortable rhythm of 2/4 breathing, let it run for about three minutes, then start the following sequence:

Concentrate on your feet. Wiggle them about. Curl them to tense the muscles, then allow them to relax.

Concentrate next on your calf muscles. Tighten and relax them.

Concentrate on your thigh muscles. Tighten and relax them.

Concentrate on your buttock muscles. Tighten your buttocks, then relax them.

Concentrate on your stomach muscles, a very common tension focus. Tighten then relax them.

Concentrate on your hands. Curl them into fists, then relax them.

Concentrate on your arms. Tighten them rigidly, then relax them.

Concentrate on your back. Tighten the muscles, then relax them.

Concentrate on your chest. Tighten the muscles, then relax them.

Concentrate on your shoulders, another very common tension focus. Hunch your shoulders to tighten the muscles, then relax them.

Concentrate on your neck. Tighten the muscles then relax them.

Concentrate on your face. Grit your teeth and contort your

features to tense up the facial muscles then relax them. Concentrate on your scalp. From to tighten the scalp muscles, then relax them.

Now tighten up every muscle in your body, holding your whole body rigid for a moment, then relax, letting go as completely as you can.

Do this final whole body sequence again, then again — three times in all. On the third time, take a really deep breath when you tense the muscles and sigh deeply — aloud — as you let the tension go.

You should be feeling nicely relaxed by now. If you left off your 2/4 breathing at the start of the relaxation sequence, pick up up again. Close your eyes and try to imagine your whole body getting heavier and heavier, as if it were turning to lead. You will find this visualisation increases your level of relaxation still further.

Enjoy the feel of relaxation for the rest of your session. But stay on the look-out. If you find tension creeping in anywhere (and you certainly will in the early days) don't let it worry you. Just tighten up the tense muscles a little more, then relax them.

# APPENDIX 2
## Special Music

The following is a list of baroque music pieces which can be used to create the peculiar state of mind which greatly aids communication with the sleeping giant.

The list is arranged alphabetically by composer.

**Bach**
Largo from the Concerto in G Minor for Flute and Strings
Aria to The Goldberg Variations
Largo from the Harpsichord Concerto in F Mino
Largo from the Solo Harpsichord Concerto in G Minor
Largo from the Solo Harpsichord Concerto in C Major
Largo from the Solo Harpsichord Concerto in F Major

**Corelli**
Largo from Concerto No. 7 in D Minor
Prelude and largo from the Concerto No. 8 in E Minor
Largo from Concerto No. 9 in A Major
Largo from Concerto No. 10 in F Major

**Handel**
Largo from Concerto No. 1 in F

Largo from Concerto No. 3 in D
Largo from Concerto No.1 in B-flat Major

**Telemann**
Largo from Double Fantasia in G Major for Harpsichord
Largo from Concerto in G Major for Viola and String Orchestra

**Vivaldi**
Largo from Winter, in The Four Seasons
Largo from Concerto in D Major for Guitar and Strings
Largo from Concerto in C Major for Mandolin, Strings and Harpsichord
Largo from Concerto in D Minor for Viola D'Amore, Strings and Harpsichord
Largo from Concerto in F Major for Viola D'Amore, Two Oboes, Bassoon, Two Horns and Figured Brass
Largo from Flute Concerto No. 4 in G Major